In her beautiful book, *The Intention Project*, Carol Streit has put together a one-of-a-kind intention journal for you to enlist the help of the Universe in creating a life more magnificent than can be imagined. Containing a unique combination of intentions, affirmations and motivational quotes, this book may just become the greatest manifestation tool you've ever used.

Janet Tyler Johnson
Author, Speaker, CFP professional, Investment Advisor, Podcast Host, and Founder of "Corporate Hostage, No More!"
www.janettylerjohnson.com
www.corporatehostagenomore.org
jtjohnson@jataj.com

The graphics, quotes and a[...] are life changing but light hea[...] is a dynamic believer in being [...] and has passionately exhibite[...] has created a valuable and u[...] who desires to change, improve or enhance their life and raise their consciousness. The book is sure to be a blessing to all who read and use it.

Pastor Debra J. Savage
B.S.N., M.A. in Religion

If you want to quickly and powerfully change your life, setting intentions for what you want is one of the most powerful ways to do so. Setting intentions changes your "I wish" into "I will," it reduces or removes obstacles such as fear and doubt, and it puts you in a place of power within your life.

Carol's book does a brilliant job of helping you cultivate the habit of setting intention so that you can create the life you've always dreamed of. I'd highly recommend it to anyone who is tired of wishing things were different and is ready to start creating the life they want.

Shayla Logan
Inspirational Speaker, Professional Fear Buster Best-Selling Author of *10 Beliefs That Are Killing Your Business*
www.shaylalogan.com

Carol is a master at the art of intention. She has transformed her life through her own will. Every change starts with an intention, and Carol's book offers an elegant and simple approach on how you can create your heart's desires based on choosing to do so! Through following Carol's simple process, you too can begin your journey of having the life that you dream of having!

Lauren Wyatt
Love Psychic & Relationship Coach
www.beelovingbeewise.com

Carol Streit has designed a beautiful and functional tool for those who walk the path of personal growth. Finding beautiful pictures, inspiring messages and useful tips on every page inspires me to take that extra step in life each and every day. I especially love the way it lets me have the freedom to come and go as I please, filling in the dates myself! As a coach, I know not everyone works the same way, and this combination of inspiration, function, and flexibility is simply divine!

Jennifer Murphy
No Limits Life Coaching
www.nolimitslifecoach.com

The Intention Project is a beautiful notebook full of inspiration that allows you to explore your whimsy within the strength of your goal development! Carol has created a magically delightful place to jot down your dreams and color outside the lines. In fact, you can draw your own lines because YOU are ultimately the creator of your thoughts and actions based on the intentions. This space is safe but it also helps to gently hold you accountable while you are shifting. Do not deny yourself the gift of opening up your mind and heart to more of what life has to give you!

Angelique Trigueros
M.S.,CCC-SLP,CPC

Maral Keuftedjian
Managing Director –
Finance at United Airlines

I'd highly recommend *The Intention Project!* My husband and I had personal experience using the intentions Carol wrote for us on how to embrace change to enhance new career and business opportunities. Every day we read the intentions, we felt better about our futures. We felt spiritual relief.

Carol lives her life embracing change, new opportunities, and new friendships without hesitation. Her book will open your eyes to many possibilities that await you and will enhance your thinking and your way of life.

If you are interested in transforming your life, then I would highly recommend using the tools in *The Intention Project*! Carol Streit is a profound intuitive coach. She has combined her genuine gifts of intuition, divine inspiration, and higher consciousness to develop a unique process that will help you create the life you desire. I believe that using Carol's approach to manifesting is a dynamic way to increase your personal power, happiness, and fulfillment!

Karen Bauer
Author of *100 Things
I Learned in Heaven*

Storm Cantwell
founder of Defense by Storm
and Creation by Design,
and inspiration for the 1989 movie,
Road House, starring Patrick Swayze.

I've known Carol Streit for nearly four years and have seen her grow, learn, adapt, and overcome in all situations she has come across, using the powerful tool of setting intentions. Now, Carol is sharing that same powerful tool with the world. *The Intention Project* shows that it truly doesn't matter what we encounter in our lives; our perspective and our choices are the critical components.

I recently met Carol and knew immediately that she's a winner. Her keen insights and life experiences have shaped her into the marvelous person she is today. Carol's ability to remain extremely focused amid life's distractions, along with her intelligence and compassion for others, made a lasting impression on me. There is no doubt that Carol and her work have made an impact on my life, and it is one I will always cherish.

Wayne L. Washington
Founder & CEO
Facility Management &
Engineering, Inc.
www.facilitymgt.com

The Intention Project

SOUL MESSAGES TO MAGICALLY TRANSFORM YOUR LIFE

CAROL STREIT

Copy Editor

Kymm Stokke

Photo Credit

Mike White of M&M Photo

Cover Design

Ruby Door Art & Design

Book Design

Ruby Door Art & Design

Proofreading

Kymm Stokke

· ·

www.growingovaries.com

Acknowledgments

It has taken a village to birth this book. I'm overwhelmed with gratitude to the people in my life who believed in me and this project.

I thank God for being my co-writer and inspiration.
You spoke to me each day through my inner guidance.
When I began to listen, it became a game changer.

At the top of the list is my husband and partner in adventure, Bob.
Who knew this brilliant and sexy man would enter my life?
I set an intention for you and was shocked at what the universe provided.
Each year with you is more special than the last.

**Thank you to my wonderful children,
Josh, Jon, Jacob, Steph, Jennie, and Jess.**
Your love touches my soul and makes me whole.
Thank you to my wonderful daughter-in-law, Rachel,
for giving me the gift of two small earth angels.
I'm excited for you as you find your way in the world.

To my sister-in-law, Karen Bauer,
a spiritual medium and author of *100 Things I Learned in Heaven*.
Your guidance and encouragement over the past few years has meant
everything to me. You envisioned the book before I did.

Thank you, Michael Mapes, for being my coach.
You have connected me to my higher self and to my purpose.
Thanks for letting me see the light of my gifts and enabling me
to bring them to the world. You have connected me to a
community of like-minded entrepreneurs.

Thank you to Stacey at Ruby Door Art & Design.
You took my vision and brought it to life through your artistic genius.
Thank you for your hard work and dedication on this project.
You may be the best graphic designer on the planet.

To Kymm Stokke, my editor.
You came into my life as my academic advisor when I went back
to college at age 55. I'm so glad that I asked for your guidance.
You "get" grammar and punctuation better than anyone else I know.

To Valerie Weber of Griffin Executive Virtual Assistants,
thank you for being on my team. You are able to juggle tons of projects
and never miss a beat. You do the things that I hate to do. You do them
so well and allow me to concentrate on creation, the thing I love.

Thanks to my extended family and friends.
You were always there for me with encouragement and support.
Thanks to my brother, Charlie. You have taught me to value family
above all. Thank you to Bob's siblings for being such an inspiration,
as I watched you attain your dreams.

Joen Larson,
thank you for opening doors for me and for helping me believe that I was
worthy of a great life. You showed me what a strong woman looks like and
walked beside me every step of the way. Love you Lohrville girl!

I have met so many incredible colleagues and peers over the past year.
Angelique Trigueros, Janet Tyler Johnson, Shayla Logan, Jennifer Murphy,
and Lauren Wyatt you inspire me every day. There are so many others not
listed here. I'm proud to call you friends.

Pastor Debra Savage, thank you for being an inspiration.
You are an earth angel that radiates love and light.
Little did I know that you would cross my path
and touch my life in a profound way.

Thank you to my fellow co-workers at Ames Laboratory.
You listened to my daily chatter about my business and upcoming book.
Never did you squash my dreams.
Thanks for being a big part of this adventure.

Maral and Vatche' Keuftedjian,
thank you for blessing my life with your gentle souls.
Words can't express the joy you have brought to me.
You have opened me up to new experiences and adventures that I cherish.
You always believed in me.

Norm Cantwell you are a gentle giant that has touched my heart.
You have inspired me with your story.
You are a true healer that has made his life purpose all about serving
others and sharing love. Thank you for teaching me in profound ways.

Thank you to Wayne Washington for being a guiding light.
Your mission to help underprivileged children touches my soul.
I so want to be a part of your vision.
You are my advocate and a big supporter of this project.

It is difficult to mention everyone that has shaped and molded me to become the person that I am today. Some of you I've known for years, others I haven't known as long. Each of you have guided me on this journey. I'm blessed to have you in my life.

This project has taught me to pay close attention to the people who come into my life. One never knows how others might guide and help.

"People come into your life for a reason, a season, or a lifetime. When you figure out which it is, you know exactly what to do."

-MICHELLE VENTOR

Dedication

The Intention Project is dedicated to my mom, Muriel Buffham Brown. She died too early of breast cancer and was never able to fulfill her passions. My vow to her is to never, ever allow that to happen to me or anyone else. Thus, my mission in life is to share my knowledge, teaching others to find their voice, live with passion, and serve others, using their gifts to make the world a better place. Mom, I've got this.

P.S. Love you mom and dad.

Foreward

WHAT'S IN AN INTENTION? ACCORDING TO CAROL STREIT . . . EVERYTHING! In *The Intention Project,* Carol shows us how setting, and fully committing to something as easy as setting an intention can shift our lives in powerful and positive ways, both imagined and unimagined. Don't believe me? That's OK; you will by the time you've completed the exercises in this book.

Having worked with thousands of entrepreneurs all around the world, I have the discernment and intuition to know when I'm in the presence of someone who is really special, and who has an idea the world needs to know about. This is how I feel about Carol Streit and her Intention Pages. Not only have I seen Carol use this process to improve her own life, over and over again, more on that in just a moment, I've also seen her use this process on behalf of others to support them in creating miraculous transformations that seemed impossible to them only days or weeks before.

Carol attended my annual live event called Wealth Creation Live. Although I didn't know it at the time, only a few days prior to the event she had no idea who I was! Several days before, she had connected with a new friend who told her about the work I do and my event. Following her intuition, Carol said "yes" to coming to the event, booked her hotel, and drove the several hours required to be in the audience. As if that wasn't a big enough leap of faith, less than 48 hours later, she said "yes" to working with me. Less than one year later this book is being published and brought to a global audience.

What I would later learn is that Carol had been using her intuition, and her intentions, to dramatically transform her life long before we ever connected. In fact, she had used the process she shares with you in this book to become an entrepreneur and leave her job, find and meet her soul mate, and find more passion and joy in her life at a time when many people feel it is just too late for them to change, choose to give up, or close their minds to new possibilities entirely.

When you first meet Carol, you can't help but be immediately drawn in by her presence, and the light that naturally emanates from within her. In *The Intention Project*, Carol's taken that light and infused it into these pages. Because what Carol understands is when you set an intention, the universe immediately sends you opportunities to see that intention take root in your life. It then becomes your job to use your intuition to see those opportunities, and to take right action that will allow those opportunities to become your new reality.

 The intentions contained in these pages started as simple Facebook posts beginning in January of 2014, and over the course of a year they grew into something much larger. Carol did not set out to write a book that shares the universal laws of spirituality and manifestation. She did not set out to write a book that would allow anyone, from novice to beginner, to architect positive changes in their life more quickly. She did not set out to write a book that would support you in unlocking more inner resourcefulness, creativity, and spiritual power than you are even currently aware you have. And yet, that's exactly what she did, and exactly what's available to you when you commit to implementing the wisdom contained herein.

Just as Carol said "yes" over and over again to making her dreams a reality, this book is about you saying "yes" to yourself. Not yes to your plan. Not yes to exactly how you think things need to look. Not yes to your fears, doubts, or imposed limitations, but yes to your highest good, yes to your most divine purpose, and yes to the most creative vision for your life. Believe me when I tell you, within this guide you'll find the exact tools you need to do just this.

Using this book in the way it was intended requires courage, conviction, and a willingness to transform yourself. If you do, your life will change, miracles will occur, profound transformation will follow you wherever you go, and you will experience more meaning, more fulfillment, and more satisfaction every single day.

How can I be so certain? It's simple… I know Carol.

From my mind to yours,
Michael Mapes, Intuitive Business Mentor

Introduction

FOR MANY YEARS, I LIVED A LIFE UNFULFILLED. My life was on autopilot. It was the usual hamster wheel existence. I went to work, did my job, had pleasant enough exchanges with my co-workers, came home, had dinner, watched a little TV, and then it was off to bed. My weekends were filled with interactions with my family and friends but then on Monday it was back to the grind.

Each day I felt as if I wasn't making a difference in the world. I felt as if my God-given talents and gifts were unused. I wasn't sure how to get out of my rut. I just knew that I needed to. Before long, days became weeks, weeks became months, and months became years.

I felt as if I was dying a little inside each day. I wanted so much more. I had big dreams that I wanted to share with the world. I knew that I had gifts that I hadn't even tapped into, but I was stuck and didn't know how to make a big change in my life. I just knew that the answer had to be somewhere.

My transformational journey began eight years ago. At age 55, I turned my life upside down and filed for divorce. The first thing I did was to check off the top two things on my goal list: college and braces. Next on the list was to date again. I was in search of my soul mate and great love. I stepped outside my comfort zone in order to live a more authentic life. I was a Baby Boomer in search of adventure, passion, and love. There would be no sitting on the porch, in a rocking chair, for me.

I signed up with an on-line dating site, wrote a catchy profile and hit "send." It took just six months before I would have my first date with Bob, my future husband. We would marry a year and a half later.

The pivotal day of my transformation was on my wedding day, August 16, 2008. Prior to that day, I would have told you that I didn't believe in mediums or messages from beyond, but when Bob's sister, Karen, channeled my mom, who had died in 1980 of breast cancer, I became a believer. Mom's message changed my life.

From that day forward I set off on a new path. I began to read and study every book I could find about spirituality and the power of intention. I listened to CDs, and watched DVDs. I attended workshops and classes. My mission was to learn everything I could. I wasn't completely sure where this newfound interest came from, but I followed my passion without second guessing myself.

I learned that everything has vibrational energy: every word, every sound, every tone, every color, every smell, every thought. I learned that we can attract things into our lives, whether positive or negative, by the positive or negative thoughts we have. There are no neutral thoughts. Every thought creates an effect in our lives.

Eventually I learned the importance of setting intentions. I became crystal clear on what I wanted. I developed written intentions for the things I wanted to manifest into my life, my Intention Pages were born. Each was specific and contained visioning exercises, preparation, affirmations, and words of gratitude. Each day I would read aloud each Intention Page.

Over time, the intentions that I set began to come true. I found my soul mate, received a promotion at work on my birthday, quit my job, became an entrepreneur, became an author, and even found my dream car. I used the practice to sell my home by setting an intention and envisioning the perfect couple buying it. It had been on the market for over five years without any nibbles, but my home sold within 30 days when I used this practice.

I had informed the universe of my intentions and the universe responded in the most amazing ways. Opportunities presented themselves to me. I seemed to be in the right place at the right time, all the time. Out of the blue, people would show up to guide and assist me. One person would lead me to another. My life began to shift and I felt more fulfilled. I started pursuing my passions.

If you have ever wanted to transform your life, it is not too late. You have the opportunity to gain access to the knowledge I accumulated over the past few years in *The Intention Project*.

The Intention Project contains 52 weekly "I Intend" statements. As you put them into practice, these simple but powerful intentions will begin to transform your life. You will begin to feel unstuck. You will find greater happiness and will feel more at peace. You will start to release any self-limiting beliefs that have held you back. You will begin to change your negative thoughts to more positive thoughts. Your vibrational energy will raise and you will be in alignment with what you want to attract into your life.

These "I Intend" statements will lead you to the larger intentions you want in life. Are you looking for your soul mate? Do you want to change careers? Would you like to stop dieting and still lose weight? Do you wish you had more abundance in the form of new opportunities, creativity, and financial freedom? The secret is based on setting intentions, applying the principles within these pages, and following through with action.

Don't live a life unfulfilled. Don't wait for your life to begin. Chart a course in a different direction, one that brings you joy.

It doesn't matter what age, background, or life experiences you have had. Today is a new day. Take charge of it. Begin to change your story and you will begin to change your life.

My coaching programs help women transform their lives. I'm especially passionate about helping Baby Boomers find their voice, passion, and purpose. Connect with me at www.growingovaries.com. Sign up for my free Dating Kit and learn the secrets of the 5-minute date.

I can't wait to connect with you. It will be at the perfect time and in the perfect way. Let's begin an adventure together.

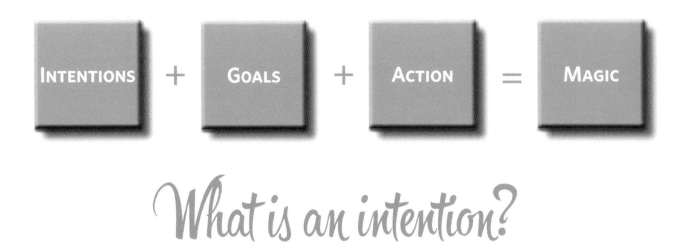

INTENTIONS + GOALS + ACTION = MAGIC

What is an intention?

Setting an intention is a powerful tool in your journey toward transformation, but an intention is useless without having a goal and developing a plan of action. An intention is the engine; the desire to reach the goal is the fuel.

An intention is a vow, a solemn promise, something to act on with dedication. If you say I intend to do something, you have already made a commitment to yourself to follow through.

Your goal is more easily achieved if it has a step-by-step plan of action, and if you set measureable dates by which to attain your goals. No one ever fulfilled her dreams without setting goals and following through with dedication and hard work.

An intention has a spiritual twist. When you inform the universe of your intention, you are asking for guidance and direction from God. The universe conspires to help you. The pieces fall into place without manipulating the outcome. You begin to notice the coincidences in your life and wonder how events happened so magically. Inspired action leads you step-by-step to the perfect outcome and the fulfillment of your goals.

Showing gratitude is an important step in fulfilling your intentions, as well as believing that your intentions have already come true. Know that everything is working on your behalf. Some of your intentions will happen quickly; others will take longer. Remember, it's a journey and not a race.

Be open to seeing all possibilities when setting your intentions. You may have specific requirements for what you want. You may see the outcome and have planned each step out according to your wishes, when in reality the universe knows what is best for you. If you aren't open to substitution you may miss out.

"Hold the vision. Trust the process."

AUTHOR UNKNOWN

How to use this book

The Intention Project contains 52 inspiring "I Intend" statements, one for each week of the year. Each playful graphic sends a powerful message that will touch your heart. Each intention contains soul messages, affirmations, and quotes. Blank calendar pages have been added to allow you to begin at any time of the year.

The intentions in this book are the first steps to living a more fulfilled life. Start at the beginning of the book or choose an intention that speaks to your soul and include it in your daily practice for the next seven days. Read aloud the "I Intend" statement and the accompanying inspirational messages each day. Journal your thoughts in the space provided, charting your journey to your best self.

Some of the photos and messages in *The Intention Project* may grip your heart more firmly. You may need to concentrate longer than a week on certain intentions. Allow yourself to pause and give the attention you need to those areas of your life. There's no hurry. As time goes by, you'll notice a greater sense of happiness and fulfillment. Your life will begin to flow more easily. You'll experience less drama, and soon, you'll look at your life and see that you've begun a transformation.

Setting intentions is magical. Start today to change your life.

Monday	Tuesday	Wednesday	Thursday

Friday	Saturday	Sunday	Birthdays

I intend to age gracefully

Aging is a privilege and one to be embraced.

Make a decision to be your best self, whatever your age.

Bask in your wisdom, grace, and beauty.

Smile often.
You have much to share with the world.

Affirmation:
I AM BEAUTIFUL IN EVERY WAY AND I EMBRACE MY AGE.

WE DELIGHT IN THE BEAUTY OF THE BUTTERFLY, BUT RARELY ADMIT THE CHANGES IT HAS GONE THROUGH TO ACHIEVE THAT BEAUTY.
MAYA ANGELOU

Date: _____

Date: _____

Date: _____

Date: _____

Date: _____

I intend to be open to change

Be open to changing the direction of your life.

Change will lead you to new opportunities and adventure.

Growth occurs when you step outside your safety zone,
doing things that are uncomfortable.

Accept the new direction of your life as you surrender to new possibilities.

Live a more satisfying life filled with new experiences and new people.

Affirmation:

I AM ACCEPTING OF CHANGE AS IT FORMS AND MOLDS MY LIFE.

None of us knows what the next change is going to be, what unexpected opportunity is just around the corner, waiting to change all the tenor of our lives.

KATHLEEN NORRIS

Date: _____

Date: _____

Date: _____

Date: _____

Date: _____

I intend to improve my relationship

If you want more love in your relationship, give more love.

Do the little things that bring joy and love.

Forgive first.

Overlook the little things.

Plan a date night.

Kiss more.

Affirmation:

OUR LOVING RELATIONSHIP IS GROWING STRONGER AND STRONGER.

Do what you did in the beginning of a relationship and there won't be an end.

ANTHONY ROBBINS

Date: _____

Date: _____

Date: _____

Date: _____

Date: _____

I intend to find my tribe

Everyone needs a tribe.
They support you when others won't.
They pull you up when things are tough.
They celebrate you and your successes.

Affirmation:
MY TRIBE SUPPORTS ME AND LOVES ME UNCONDITIONALLY.

Surround yourself with the dreamers and the doers, the believers and the thinkers, but most of all, surround yourself with those who see the greatness within you, even when you don't see it yourself.

EDMUND LEE

Date: _____

_____

_____

_____

Date: _____

_____

_____

_____

Date: _____

_____

_____

_____

Date: _____

_____

_____

_____

Date: _____

_____

_____

_____

Monday	Tuesday	Wednesday	Thursday

Friday	Saturday	Sunday	Birthdays

I intend to change my story

Everyone has a story.
Change your story and you will change your life.
Release any attachment to your past.
Send love and forgiveness to anyone who has caused you pain.

Affirmation:
I RELEASE MY PAST AND AM OPEN TO CHANGING MY STORY.

Your story may not have such a happy beginning, but that doesn't make you who you are. It is the rest of your story, who you choose to be . . .

SOOTHSAYER FROM KUNG FU PANDA

Date: _____

_____
_____
_____

Date: _____

_____
_____
_____

Date: _____

_____
_____
_____

Date: _____

_____
_____
_____

Date: _____

_____
_____
_____

A smile is a universal language that is meant to touch many hearts.

Share your smile with someone today.

Not only will you make someone's day but you will feel better too.

One smile can make all the difference in someone's life.

Affirmation:
I AM ABUNDANTLY BLESSED AND JOYFUL. MY SMILE HAS MADE A DIFFERENCE IN SOMEONE'S LIFE TODAY.

WE SHALL NEVER KNOW ALL THE GOOD THAT A SIMPLE SMILE CAN DO.

MOTHER TERESA

Date: _____

Date: _____

Date: _____

Date: _____

Date: _____

I intend to give up control

Release the need to control everything in your life.

Be open to allowing the universe to guide you.

Sometimes the best journeys are those without a plan.

A new direction may lead to new opportunities and adventures.

Trust and believe.

Affirmation:

I AM OPEN TO RELEASING CONTROL AND ALLOWING MY DIVINE PLAN TO ENSUE.

You can't control everything. Sometimes you just need to relax and have faith that things will work out. Let go a little and just let life happen.

KODY KEPLINGER

Date: _____

_____

_____

_____

Date: _____

_____

_____

_____

Date: _____

_____

_____

_____

Date: _____

_____

_____

_____

Date: _____

_____

_____

_____

I intend to have no regrets

Live life with no regret.

Let there be no "could haves" or "should haves" in your life.

Take chances and follow your dreams.

Make mistakes

Live your life.

Affirmation:

I RELAX IN MY DECISIONS AND MOVE ON WITH CONFIDENCE.

Accept everything about yourself – I mean everything, you are you and that is the beginning and the end – no apologies, no regrets.

HENRY A. KISSINGER

Date: _____

Date: _____

Date: _____

Date: _____

Date: _____

Monday	Tuesday	Wednesday	Thursday

Friday	Saturday	Sunday	Birthdays

Life was not meant to be taken so seriously.

Each day take time to do something fun.

Chart a new territory.

Take a risk.

Affirmation:

MY LIFE IS FILLED WITH LAUGHTER AND TIME TO PLAY.

The great man is he who does not lose his child's heart.

MENCIOUS

Date:_____

Date:_____

Date:_____

Date:_____

Date:_____

I intend to be responsible

You have control of your life and your happiness. Stop blaming others. Be responsible for your own life. Be your authentic self. Live your authentic life.

Affirmation:

TODAY I CHANGE MY LIFE BY TAKING RESPONSIBILITY. I AM IN CONTROL OF MY LIFE.

Accept responsibility for your life. Know that it is you who will get you where you want to go, no one else.

LES BROWN

Date:_____

Date:_____

Date:_____

Date:_____

Date:_____

I intend to heal my past

Don't allow your past to define you.

Take time to acknowledge and respect your past wounds.

Allow healing.

Let go of what no longer serves you.

Live fully in the present.

Affirmation:

I AM MAKING PEACE WITH MY PAST AND NOW FOCUS ON TODAY.

WE DO NOT HEAL THE PAST BY DWELLING THERE; WE HEAL THE PAST BY LIVING FULLY IN THE PRESENT.

-MARIANNE WILLIAMSON

Date: _____

Date: _____

Date: _____

Date: _____

Date: _____

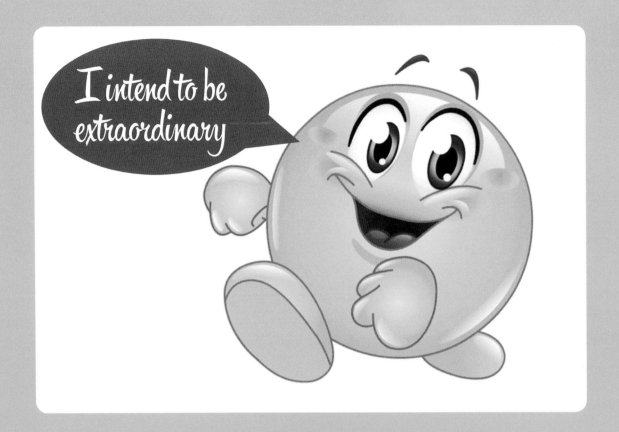

Look for opportunities in everything.

Have fun in your life and break some rules.

Be the best version of yourself.

Be a dreamer.

Be a doer.

Affirmation:
TODAY, I SEE MYSELF AS EXTRAORDINARY.

We have one precious life: do something extraordinary today, even if it's tiny. A pebble starts the avalanche.

K.A. LAITY

Date: _____

Date: _____

Date: _____

Date: _____

Date: _____

Monday	Tuesday	Wednesday	Thursday

Friday	Saturday	Sunday	Birthdays

I intend to hug more

Hugs are universal medicine.

They reduce stress and dissolve anger.

They put broken pieces back together.

Hugs are love without words.

Affirmation:

MY SIMPLE HEARTFELT HUGS ARE A GIFT TO THE WORLD.

A hug is a handshake from the heart.

AUTHOR UNKNOWN

Date: _____

Date: _____

Date: _____

Date: _____

Date: _____

Appreciate the ordinary moments and experiences in each day.

Take your focus off of tomorrow and live today with deep meaning.

Give thanks for today's gifts.

Make today your favorite day.

Affirmation:
I APPRECIATE THE GIFT OF TODAY AND CELEBRATE THE LITTLE THINGS IN LIFE.

Do what you can, with what you have, where you are.

THEODORE ROOSEVELT

Date: _____

Date: _____

Date: _____

Date: _____

Date: _____

I intend to enjoy the journey

Life is not a race, but a journey.

Always take the scenic route.

Each day is an adventure.

Appreciate the ride.

Affirmation:
I EMBRACE AND TRUST MY JOURNEY.

IT IS GOOD TO HAVE AN END TO JOURNEY TOWARD; BUT IT IS THE JOURNEY THAT MATTERS, IN THE END.

ERNEST HEMINGWAY

Date: _____

Date: _____

Date: _____

Date: _____

Date: _____

I intend to
pay attention

Spirit is trying to communicate with you every day.

All you need to do is pay attention and listen to your intuition.

Use these clues as guides to direct your life.

Each is significant.

Affirmation:
EACH DAY I PAY
ATTENTION AND
FOLLOW MY INTUITION.

I think the one lesson I
have learned is that
there is no substitute
for paying attention.

DIANE SAWYER

Date: _____

Date: _____

Date: _____

Date: _____

Date: _____

Monday	Tuesday	Wednesday	Thursday

Friday	Saturday	Sunday	Birthdays

I intend to be proud of me

You have many things to be proud of.

You have accomplished much.

Your life has touched many lives.

There is nothing you can't be or do.

Be proud of you.

Affirmation:

I AM PROUD OF THE PERSON I HAVE BECOME AND LOVE MYSELF UNCONDITIONALLY.

Success to me is being happy, truly fulfilled, being proud of myself, and doing different things all the time.

LEIGHTON MEESTER

Date: _____

Date: _____

Date: _____

Date: _____

Date: _____

Anger raises your blood pressure and affects your health.

Anger shortens your life.

Release any anger you feel.

Take a deep breath and relax.

See the situation differently.

Affirmation:
TODAY I RELEASE MY ANGER AND FORGIVE THOSE WHO MAKE ME ANGRY.

For every minute you remain angry, you give up sixty seconds of peace of mind.

RALPH WALDO EMERSON

Date: _____

Date: _____

Date: _____

Date: _____

Date: _____

I intend to change direction

It's never too late to choose a new direction.
It doesn't matter at what stage of life you are.
A world of opportunity is waiting for you.
Steer your course today.

Affirmation:

I AM OPEN TO THE OPPORTUNITIES THAT COME FROM CHANGING MY DIRECTION.

ROWING HARDER DOESN'T HELP IF THE BOAT IS HEADED IN THE WRONG DIRECTION.

KENICHI OHMAE

Date: _____

Date: _____

Date: _____

Date: _____

Date: _____

I intend to
think less

Stop overthinking things.

Stop pushing, pulling, and manipulating the outcome.

Start going where you are guided.

Start surrendering to the outcome.

Affirmation:

I FIND NEW HAPPINESS
BY THINKING LESS AND
LIVING MORE.

Get out of your head
and get into your heart.
Think less, feel more.

OSHO

Date: _____

Date: _____

Date: _____

Date: _____

Date: _____

Monday	Tuesday	Wednesday	Thursday

Friday	Saturday	Sunday	Birthdays

I intend to anticipate life

Anticipate the good things in life.

Play like there's no tomorrow.

Enjoy the sunshine on your face.

Spend time with friends and family.

Affirmation:

TODAY I AWAKEN IN ANTICIPATION THAT SOMETHING WONDERFUL WILL HAPPEN.

Anticipate the day as if it was your birthday and you were turning six again.

MIKE DOLAN

Date: _____

Date: _____

Date: _____

Date: _____

Date: _____

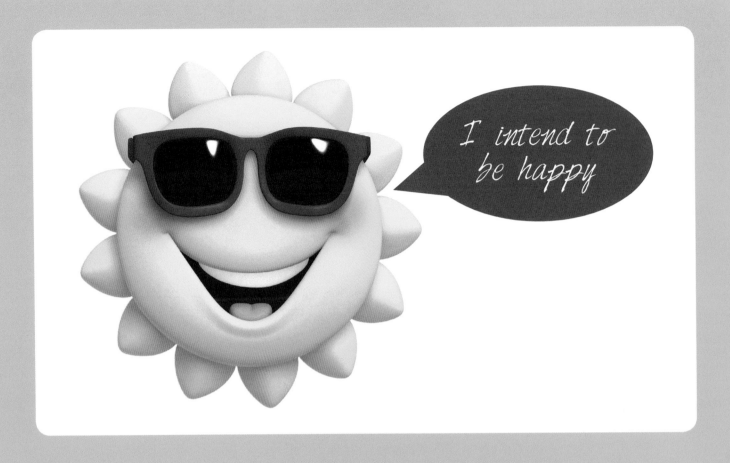

Good morning sunshine!
You are a ray of hope.
You make a difference in someone's life.
Concentrate on other's happiness and happiness
will find you.

Affirmation:

**I HAVE ALL I NEED TO BE HAPPY
AND MAKE TODAY AMAZING.**

Happiness cannot be traveled
to, owned, earned, or worn.
It is the spiritual experience
of living every minute with
love, grace & gratitude.

DENIS WAITLEY

Date:_____

_____

_____

_____

Date:_____

_____

_____

_____

Date:_____

_____

_____

_____

Date:_____

_____

_____

_____

Date:_____

_____

_____

_____

I intend to communicate better

What you say is important and needs to be shared.

No one will know what you want unless you tell them.

You can't expect people to read your mind.

When you make your wishes known,
the Universe responds.

Affirmation:
I AM VOICING MY OPINIONS
AND STANDING UP FOR WHAT
I WANT AND BELIEVE IN.

IT TOOK ME QUITE A LONG
TIME TO DEVELOP A VOICE,
AND NOW THAT I HAVE IT, I
AM NOT GOING TO BE SILENT.

MADELEINE ALBRIGHT

Date: _____

_____

_____

_____

Date: _____

_____

_____

_____

Date: _____

_____

_____

_____

Date: _____

_____

_____

_____

Date: _____

_____

_____

_____

I intend to love more

Everyone wants more love in her life.

That love could come from loving yourself more,
having deep relationships with family and friends,
from a spouse or partner, or from meeting someone new.

In order to get more love, give more love.

Release all fears about love.

Affirmation:
I AM WORTHY OF LOVE AND LOVE MYSELF UNCONDITIONALLY.

Love is the master key that opens the gates of happiness.

OLIVER WENDELL HOLMES

Date: _____

Date: _____

Date: _____

Date: _____

Date: _____

Monday	Tuesday	Wednesday	Thursday

| Friday | Saturday | Sunday | Birthdays |

I intend to make my own decisions

You know exactly what you want.

You do not make decisions lightly.

Your decisions are based on years of experience and knowledge.

Don't worry that someone isn't going to like your decision.

Affirmation:

I CHOOSE TO MAKE MY OWN DECISIONS AND KNOW EXACTLY WHAT IS BEST FOR ME.

I am my own person capable of making my own decisions and choosing powerfully how I live.

MIRANDA KERR

Date: _____

Date: _____

Date: _____

Date: _____

Date: _____

I intend to see today's magic

Fulfillment doesn't come from your title
or where you live.
Fulfillment comes from today and now.
Seek new adventures and people.
Grow. Expand. Reach.

Affirmation:
**I AM EMBRACING THE
UNKNOWN, SEEKING THE
EXCITEMENT OF TODAY.**

*Learn from yesterday, live for
today, hope for tomorrow.
The important thing is not to
stop questioning.*

ALBERT EINSTEIN

Date: _____

Date: _____

Date: _____

Date: _____

Date: _____

I intend to follow inspired action

Journal your ideas.

Consciously follow where you are led.

Let your ideas flow.

Ask that you be directed clearly and consciously.

Affirmation:

NEW OPPORTUNITIES COME TO ME WHEN I FOLLOW THROUGH WITH INSPIRED ACTION.

LUCK IS TRULY WHERE PREPARATION MEETS OPPORTUNITY.

RANDY PAUSCH

Date: _____

Date: _____

Date: _____

Date: _____

Date: _____

I intend to not be jealous

Have no feelings of jealousy, envy, or judgment toward others.

As you treat others, you treat yourself.

As you think ill thoughts, you send ill thoughts to yourself.

Send love and blessings to everyone.

Affirmation:

I RELEASE MY THOUGHTS OF JEALOUSY AND HAVE FAITH IN MYSELF.

Don't waste your time on jealousy. Sometimes you're ahead, sometimes you're behind. The race is long, and in the end, it's only with yourself.

BAZ LUHRMANN

Date: _____

Date: _____

Date: _____

Date: _____

Date: _____

Monday	Tuesday	Wednesday	Thursday

Friday	Saturday	Sunday	Birthdays

I intend
to not
settle

Don't settle for a life unfulfilled.

Believe that you can have
what you really want.

Choosing good enough over great is settling.

You will know in your heart
the correct path to choose.

Affirmation:

**I AM DESERVING OF A
LIFE FILLED WITH LOVE,
JOY, AND SATISFACTION.**

If you don't know what you want,
you'll never find it. If you don't know
what you deserve, you'll always
settle for less. You will wander
aimlessly, uncomfortably numb in
your comfort zone, wondering how
life has ended up here.

ROB LIANO

Date: _____

Date: _____

Date: _____

Date: _____

Date: _____

I intend to sleep soundly

Release all thoughts that you are struggling with.

Know that you did your best.

Send love and blessings to anyone who caused you pain.

Concentrate on happy thoughts.

Affirmation:
I AM ABLE TO SLEEP SOUNDLY AS I RELEASE MY NEGATIVE THOUGHTS.

Sleep is the best meditation.

DALAI LAMA

Date:_____

Date:_____

Date:_____

Date:_____

Date:_____

I intend to be creative

Creativity takes many shapes.

Make mistakes.

Be courageous.

Use your imagination.

Affirmation:
I AM INSPIRED EVERY DAY WITH NEW CREATIVITY THAT BRINGS ME JOY.

YOU CAN'T USE UP CREATIVITY. THE MORE YOU USE, THE MORE YOU HAVE.

MAYA ANGELOU

Date: _____

Date: _____

Date: _____

Date: _____

Date: _____

I intend to enjoy the little things

The little things quietly touch us each day.

It's up to us to notice.

We decide their importance.

Slow down and pay attention.

Affirmation:

I COUNT MY MANY BLESSINGS AND AM GRATEFUL FOR THE LITTLE THINGS IN MY LIFE.

Enjoy the little things in life because one day you'll look back and realize they were the big things.

ROBERT BRAULT

Date: _____

Date: _____

Date: _____

Date: _____

Date: _____

Monday	Tuesday	Wednesday	Thursday

Friday	Saturday	Sunday	Birthdays

I intend to
trust in my
mistakes

Only with failure will I succeed.

If I'm not failing, I'm not moving ahead.

Don't look down.

Don't look behind.

Look ahead at the prize.

Affirmation:

I AM NOT PERFECT AND WILL
MAKE MISTAKES. I TRUST IN
MY MISTAKES AND CONTINUE
TO MAKE PROGRESS TOWARD
MY GOAL.

Our greatest glory is
not in never failing,
but in rising up every
time we fail.

RALPH WALDO EMERSON

Date:_____

Date:_____

Date:_____

Date:_____

Date:_____

I intend to capitalize on my gifts

My gifts are uniquely mine and mine alone.
Each is a natural talent and strength.

As I utilize these gifts to serve others,
the doors of opportunity open to me.

Each day I brighten the world,
spreading love and peace.

Affirmation:
I AM BLESSED WITH MANY GIFTS THAT I SHARE WITH THE WORLD.

The meaning of life is to find your gift. The purpose of life is to give it away.

PABLO PICASSO

Date: _____

Date: _____

Date: _____

Date: _____

Date: _____

*I intend
to reduce
my stress*

Reduce the drama in your life.

Spend time alone doing things you love.

Interact with people who lift you up.

Change your focus.

Affirmation:
I RELEASE THE PEOPLE AND
SITUATIONS IN MY LIFE THAT
CAUSE ME STRESS.

I PROMISE YOU NOTHING IS AS
CHAOTIC AS IT SEEMS. NOTHING IS
WORTH DIMINISHING YOUR HEALTH.
NOTHING IS WORTH POISONING
YOURSELF INTO STRESS, ANXIETY,
AND FEAR.

STEVE MARABOLI

Date: _____

Date: _____

Date: _____

Date: _____

Date: _____

You have much to say and share.

You serve no one by keeping quiet.

Speak your mind.

Let us hear your voice.

Affirmation:

I AM READY TO SHARE
MY VOICE WITH THE
WORLD. IT IS MY TIME.

You have gifts to give to
the world. Find your
voice and prosper.

BEVERLY MAHONE

Date: _____

Date: _____

Date: _____

Date: _____

Date: _____

Monday	Tuesday	Wednesday	Thursday

Friday	Saturday	Sunday	Birthdays

I intend to change my thoughts

Your thoughts and words form your life.

Negative thoughts produce negative experiences.

Concentrate on having positive thoughts.

Make the most of today.

Affirmation:

TODAY IS PERFECT AND EVERYTHING IS FALLING INTO PLACE.

All that we are is the result of what we have thought. The mind is everything. What we think we become.

BUDDAH

Date:_____

Date:_____

Date:_____

Date:_____

Date:_____

I intend to reduce drama

Drama brings more drama.
What you allow is what continues.
Allow peace to flow to the situation.
Fill your heart with positive expectations.

Affirmation:
I AM NO LONGER THE
CENTER OF DRAMA.
I SET POSITIVE INTENTIONS
IN EVERY SITUATION.

If you're tired of drama
in your life, just quit
being the actor.

- WILSON KANADI

Date:_____

Date:_____

Date:_____

Date:_____

Date:_____

I intend to overcome my fear

Face your fears each day.
Move one step closer to your dream.
Let your faith be bigger than your fear.
All you have to do is take the first step.
That step leads to victory.

Affirmation:
I HAVE THE COURAGE
TO FACE MY FEARS.
I AM MORE POWERFUL
THAN FEAR.

YOU GAIN STRENGTH, COURAGE,
AND CONFIDENCE BY EVERY
EXPERIENCE IN WHICH YOU REALLY
STOP TO LOOK FEAR IN THE FACE.
YOU MUST DO THE THING WHICH
YOU THINK YOU CANNOT DO.

ELEANOR ROOSEVELT

Date: _____

Date: _____

Date: _____

Date: _____

Date: _____

There will never be another you.

Love everything that makes you special.

Show the world your true self.

Show your uniqueness.

Be you.

Affirmation:

I ACKNOWLEDGE AND SHARE MY AUTHENTIC SELF WITH THE WORLD.

Be yourself. Everyone else is already taken.

-Oscar Wilde

Date: _____

Date: _____

Date: _____

Date: _____

Date: _____

Monday	Tuesday	Wednesday	Thursday

Friday	Saturday	Sunday	Birthdays

Life is a process of learning.

Expand your mind with new ideas and experiences.

Seek knowledge and doors will open for you.

Be curious each day.

Affirmation:

I SEEK KNOWLEDGE AND DISCOVER ENDLESS POSSIBILITIES.

Anyone who stops learning is old, whether at twenty or eighty. Anyone who keeps learning stays young.

HENRY FORD

Date: _____

Date: _____

Date: _____

Date: _____

Date: _____

I intend to seek adventure

You live in a magnificent world filled with adventure.
Discover these adventures with open eyes.
Seek new experiences in your daily life.
Wear big boots every day.

Affirmation:
MY DAILY LIFE IS FILLED WITH
EXCITING OPPORTUNITIES AND
ADVENTURES.

When you see someone putting
on their big boots, you can be
pretty sure that an adventure
is going to happen.

A.A. MILNE

Date:_____

Date:_____

Date:_____

Date:_____

Date:_____

Only say "Yes" to the things that matter.

Pleasing everyone is impossible.

Say "No" without feeling guilty.

"No" is a complete sentence.

Affirmation:

I GRACIOUSLY SAY "NO" WHEN I DON'T WANT TO DO SOMETHING.

WHEN YOU SAY "YES" TO OTHERS, MAKE SURE YOU ARE NOT SAYING "NO" TO YOURSELF.

-PAULO COEHLO

Date: _____

Date: _____

Date: _____

Date: _____

Date: _____

Find the courage to ask for what you want.

Be specific and graciously ask.

It's okay if you don't have all the answers.

Believe in yourself.

Affirmation:

NEW OPPORTUNITIES ARE WAITING FOR ME WHEN I AM OPEN TO ASKING.

If you don't go after what you want, you'll never have it. If you don't ask, the answer is always no. If you don't step forward, you're always in the same place.

NORA ROBERTS

Date: _____

_____

_____

_____

Date: _____

_____

_____

_____

Date: _____

_____

_____

_____

Date: _____

_____

_____

_____

Date: _____

_____

_____

_____

Monday	Tuesday	Wednesday	Thursday

Friday	Saturday	Sunday	Birthdays

I intend to follow my dreams

Nothing ever happens overnight.

Everything worthwhile takes hard work and dedication.

In order to reach success,
you must blaze through fear and the unknown.

Set your sights on the stars.

Affirmation:

I HAVE A PLAN AND KNOW EXACTLY HOW TO ACHIEVE MY DREAMS.

A dream written down with a date becomes a goal. A goal broken down into steps becomes a plan. A plan backed by action makes your dreams come true.

GREG S. REID

Date: _____

Date: _____

Date: _____

Date: _____

Date: _____

I intend to serve

The secret to a happy life is to live a life of service.

Use your many talents to make a difference in the world.

Value others and touch someone's life.

Be humble. Be caring. Be loving.

Affirmation:
I LIVE A JOYFUL LIFE OF SERVICE USING MY MANY TALENTS AND GIFTS.

The best way to find yourself is to lose yourself in the service of others.

MAHATMA GANDHI

Date:_____

Date:_____

Date:_____

Date:_____

Date:_____

Remove clutter from your home, office, and life.

Have nothing that you no longer use or need.

Simplify things to attract new energy and opportunities into your life.

Let go of what is holding you back.

Affirmation:

MY LIFE IS SIMPLIFIED AND FREE FROM CLUTTER.

CLUTTER IS NOT JUST THE STUFF ON YOUR FLOOR – IT'S ANYTHING THAT STANDS BETWEEN YOU AND THE LIFE YOU WANT TO BE LIVING.

PETER WALSH

Date: _____

Date: _____

Date: _____

Date: _____

Date: _____

I intend to play big

Believe that you are deserving of a big life,
full of opportunities and joy.

Don't hide your magnificence.

You are perfect the way you are.

Never let fear hold you back.

Affirmation:

I HAVE CONFIDENCE IN
MY SELF-WORTH AND
PLAY BIG IN MY LIFE.

There is no passion to be found
playing small – in settling
for a life that is less than the one
you are capable of living.

NELSON MANDELA

Date: _____

Date: _____

Date: _____

Date: _____

Date: _____

Monday	Tuesday	Wednesday	Thursday

Friday	Saturday	Sunday	Birthdays

Make an impact on the world in your unique way.

Never be afraid to stand out.

Let your brilliance shine.

No more sitting back,
waiting for others to be the leader.

It's your time.

Affirmation:

**I AM AUTHENTICALLY
ME AND STAND OUT.**

The hardest challenge
is to be yourself in a
world where everyone
is trying to make you
be somebody else.

E.E. CUMMINGS

Date:_____

Date:_____

Date:_____

Date:_____

Date:_____

I intend to learn from others

Each person who touches your life has something to teach you.

Your task is to seek that knowledge.

Be open to learning something new.

Expand your world.

Affirmation:
I CHOOSE TO LEARN AND GAIN INSIGHT FROM OTHERS.

Everyone you will ever meet knows something you don't.

BILL NYE

Date:_____

_____

_____

_____

Date:_____

_____

_____

_____

Date:_____

_____

_____

_____

Date:_____

_____

_____

_____

Date:_____

_____

_____

_____

Listen to what someone is saying to you.

Can you feel their pain or understand the depth of their experience?

Forget what you were going to say.

Forget how you wanted the conversation to go.

Listen. Really listen.

Affirmation:

I COMPASSIONATELY LISTEN TO UNDERSTAND.

THERE IS A DIFFERENCE BETWEEN TRULY LISTENING AND WAITING FOR YOUR TURN TO TALK.

RALPH WALDO EMERSON

Date: _____

Date: _____

Date: _____

Date: _____

Date: _____

I intend to travel more

There is an amazing world waiting to be explored.

Plan new adventures that bring you delight.

Experience new foods, cultures, and people.

Let your heart be your guide.

Affirmation:

MY LIFE IS FILLED WITH EXCITING TRAVEL EXPERIENCES TO NEW DESTINATIONS.

Oh the places you'll go.
Today is your day!
Your mountain is waiting.
So . . . get on your way!

DR. SEUSS

Date: _____

_____

_____

_____

Date: _____

_____

_____

_____

Date: _____

_____

_____

_____

Date: _____

_____

_____

_____

Date: _____

_____

_____

_____

About the author

· ·

Carol Streit, founder of Growing Ovaries, loves to help Baby Boomers transform their lives. She inspires women to believe it's never too late to live a life filled with love, passion, and purpose. She's mom to six adult children and Oma to two awesome grandsons. She lives in Iowa with her hunky husband and soul mate, Bob. Together they love travel, adventure, and rock and roll. Connect with the author at www.growingovaries. com.

Thank you!

· ·

Thank you to my readers for allowing me to lead you on a transformational journey. May *The Intention Project* inspire you to realize that it's never too late to change your life. You are a gift that needs to be shared with the planet. You are beautiful, talented, and smart beyond measure. Each of you has a voice that needs to be heard and a soul that needs to be shared.

Thank you for believing in me and in being my support system. *The Intention Project* wasn't on my radar a year ago. The idea kept bubbling up and I ignored it for a long time. As the year progressed, I began to put the pieces together and in the process found my purpose. If I can do it, you can too.

Notes

_You are on
the right track!_

Go for it!
You can do this!

Play big!
Trust your intuition!

Manifest!
Share your knowledge!

Let your light shine!

Help others succeed!

Why not you?

Everything is perfect!
You are worthy!

_____

_____

_____

_____

_____

_____

_____

_____

_____

_____

_____

_____

_____

You are powerful beyond measure!

_You will get everything
your heart desires!_

Doors are quickly opening for you!

Find your bliss!

Keep moving forward!

When you share your gifts,
you will be abundantly rewarded!

You are loved!
You are perfect!
You are amazing!

No worries!